THE NEPTUNE EFFECT

THE
NEPTUNE
EFFECT

PATRICIA MORIMANDO

Introduction by Charles Jayne

Samuel Weiser, Inc.
York Beach, Maine

First published 1979 by

Samuel Weiser, Inc.
P.O. Box 612
York Beach, Maine 03910

Second printing 1983

ISBN 0-87728-487-3

© Patricia Morimando 1979

Printed in the U.S.A. by
Mitchell-Shear, Inc.
Ann Arbor, MI 48104

Contents

Dedication

This book is dedicated to my Virgo friends who had enough confidence in me until I found my own, and my Aries friends who shoved and badgered me until I found the courage to try. Thanks.

Introduction

This is an excellent book on the planet Neptune, the best
one that I know of. It is significant, too, since this planet has so
much to do with the relationship of people (astrologers or the
general believing public) to astrology. Nearly 45 years ago Carl
Payne Tobey, a leading astrostatistical research astrologer, made
a study of orders for astrological services received by Clancey
Publications. He found that Neptune was the main factor. As
noted by him, Elizabeth Aldrich was the first astrologer to write
knowledgeably about this elusive planet. Tobey himself wrote the
next good booklet on Neptune. Now we are fortunate to have this
third and best one in the evolution of our understanding of this
mysterious planet. The great Morinus, three centuries ago in
France, connected astrology with Mercury. Early in the twentieth
century, Alfred Witte of Germany linked astrology with Mercury-
Uranus. I find the best study that of Arthur M. Young of the
Foundation for the Study of Consciousness, who finds that most
astrologers have Mercury-Neptune combinations.

Few people would disagree as to the parlous state of our
planet due to humankind. Many may agree, also, that there is

one broad, even polyglot and heterogeneous movement that is the sole hope for us: the great consciousness-expanding movement. It has many components, and on its surface floats a lot of junk and phoniness. Psychiatry, Yoga, Astrology, Transcendental Meditation, Spiritual Healing, Theosophy, Adult Education, etc., are some of its many parts. We have lost touch with the Higher Worlds that were not so alien to the ancients. The great Carl Jung titled one of his books *Modern Man in Search of a Soul,* which is one of the best and most significant titles of our time. The author of this gem of a book on Neptune is a student of Jungian psychology and thus a vital part of this search of mankind for renewal.

In almost every case that my wife and I have seen of the horoscopes of people in this movement, one or more of the three "new" planets, i.e., Uranus, Neptune, Pluto, are major in their patterns. 1981 will mark the two-hundredth anniversary of the discovery of Uranus so, after all this time, we astrologers (with all of our shortcomings) finally know something about that planet. But with Neptune and Pluto, as yet we know all too little. One can see Uranus if one has perfect sight and under ideal seeing conditions, and one can live out its 84-year cycle, but neither of these are true of Neptune and Pluto. Therefore, anyone who can improve our understanding of them is rendering us a service considerably greater than they may realize! As Dane Rudhyar has so often and so eloquently put it, these planets symbolise the energies of Jung's Collective Unconscious. If we are to become the receiving cocreators of the Higher, and in so doing find our own salvation, we must broaden the scope of our consciousness. And to do that, in turn, means that we must learn to bring at least some of the contents of the unconscious into consciousness.

After three decades as a consultant astrologer I think I can say that those in this polychrome vanguard of mankind not only have these three outer planets prominent in their chart patterns, but also that most of them do not handle these "new" energies too well. Yet what else is to be expected since they are striving to do what are, for most of us, "new things"? It is more crucially valuable to human welfare that the new frontiers, no longer physical ones, be endeavored, even if imperfectly, than that the "old" be done relatively well. How can we best learn to handle the subtle and intense energies of Neptune and Pluto unless we have people like Pat Morimando to show us the way? Personally, I cannot conceive of anything in astrology that could be more useful than some way to improve our response to the energies of these planets, for through them our awareness is broadened from the narrowly personal and is deepened and made more sensitive.

Neptune was discovered by astronomer Galle on September 23, 1846 at 26° of the sign Aquarius as a result of brilliant computations by LeVerrier of France (paralleled by Adams in England). I have come to the conclusion that the Cosmic Center beyond our own little Planetary System, for which Neptune acts as a step-down transformer, is in Cygnus on the Galactic Equator. When Cygnus is projected down onto the ecliptic from far above, it is at approximately 24° of the sign Aquarius, and so Neptune was discovered when near this Center. I suggest that my colleagues might test this hypothesis.

Charles Jayne
Monroe, N.Y.
July 10, 1979

Preface

Men at some time are masters of their fates:
The fault, dear Brutus, is not in our stars,
But in ourselves . . . .

—Shakespeare's *Julius Caesar*
Act I, Scene II

Cause and Effect

Many of us prefer to think of ourselves as victims; that all our vicissitudes, trials, tribulations and most of our illnesses are the result of some magical, mysterious, spiritual or cosmic influence; that "it" comes from outside ourselves. Maybe "it" does. Then again, maybe it doesn't. Probably it doesn't. If I say I'm a difficult person because Saturn squares my Sun, does this excuse my behavior? Or do I at some time in my life take responsibility in reorienting my attitudes and behavior, if only to give myself surcease from pain and suffering? Am I a victim or am I the creator of my own sense of frustration? What is the cause, but more importantly *who* is the effector?

Foreword

*T*HE NEPTUNE EFFECT is written for the practicing astrologer and the advanced astrology student. It isn't intended as an astrology lesson. A well-grounded knowledge of astrology as well as a more-than-passing familiarity with human behavior and motivation, psychology, are essential due to the nature of the material contained herein. Otherwise there will be a distinct proclivity for the reader to go off the deep end and misuse the information. A certain amount of misinterpretation of the material is, however, unavoidable.

I strongly urge that this information be used responsibly. If not, harm can be done. A person undergoing a strong Neptune transit is in a highly sensitized and vulnerable state and therefore susceptible to suggestion. Experience has shown me in quite vivid terms the harm that can be done by well-intentioned "advice."

Someone asked me after one of my lectures on this subject, "How do you *tell* this to someone who's going through a Neptune transit?" My answer was, and still is, "You don't tell them. You let them tell you. This information is for you so that you'll have an idea of what that person is experiencing before they contact you; so you won't be taken off guard; so you won't make matters worse because you lack insight into the transit. That's what you *do* with this information."

Sometimes, simply allowing a person undergoing a Neptune transit to talk about what's happening on the inner level releases the built-up psychic tension and alleviates some of the confusion being experienced. If, for example, a person with Neptune transiting natal Mercury tells you "I hear voices" and you can assure them this isn't unusual during this type of transit, he or she will feel some relief. The relief is brought about by the knowledge that "hearing voices at this time" isn't abnormal. For it's the fear of an abnormality that produces the psychic tension.

Or, let us say a client begins describing symptoms of a Neptune transit to natal Mercury but is afraid to be specific due to a fear of being misunderstood. The counselor can gently prod by asking appropriate questions or making appropriate comments. To say to a client "It isn't *unusual* to hear voices under this transit . . ." allows the client to pick up the ball if he or she so chooses. This sort of gentle prodding very often opens up a reluctant person and allows the expression of the experience without fear of being misjudged.

If the counselor and client both have some understanding of the potentials of a Neptune transit, much tragedy can be avoided. The Neptune experience itself can't be avoided, however, any more than weather can be avoided. It's a matter of knowledge and response. If you know ahead of time what the weather is going to be like you have the option of preparing for it. If you must go out into bad weather you will experience inconveniences but at least you can meet most contingencies if you have prepared yourself to the best of your ability.

We each experience our own experience and that is one thing that can never be avoided. As astrologers we "see" things to come in a chart and too many of us become overly concerned about "how to tell the client" or with "should I tell the client?" I've often asked myself "Why do I want to tell the client?" and found some unsettling answers to *that* question.

No one can give anyone the answers. The answers come from experience and they are quite individual. The best any astrologer or counselor can do is to prepare a client in as positive a way as possible. We can never tell anyone what will occur—we fool ourselves and we negatively program the client if we do this. But we can say "*If* you find yourself feeling low energy. . ." or "*If* you feel confused about. . ." and then go on to recommend possible alternatives and constructive channeling of the energies. But this thing of "prediction" is always a big IF.

I'd be a fool not to admit that in certain cases an astute astrologer can call a shot with fair accuracy. In the case of a client with a history of chronic depression or a client known to be predisposed to any number of behavioral problems, the transits can and do show the timing of problematic episodes in the life. In the case of a chronic depressive it is usually wise to inform the person that a "depressive cycle" may be coming in and then go on to discuss what channels may be used during the cycle and also let him or her know the duration of the cycle. Very often the knowledge of when the cycle ends can be of immeasurable help.

However, in the case of depressive Neptune transits I don't think for a moment it's at all wise to tell someone they'll be coping with depression for a number of years! This will only increase anxiety. What is needed in this case is a discussion of an attitude adjustment for the purpose of meeting the energy—to get the person on the road to examining his or her responses to life in general. This may require in-depth counseling.

Clients coming to you on a Neptune transit or those who have one coming up can be encouraged to begin one of the many analytical programs available. They should be encouraged to read material relevant to their experience. This is the time when analysis can be most beneficial because the unconscious is quite active and receptive in most cases. It's certainly a way of constructively channeling the Neptunian energy. Other suggestions for handling a Neptune transit can be found in *Some Practical Guidelines to a Perplexing Transit* in the back of the book.

♆

The effects of Neptune are very much maligned by our Western society. When it comes to Neptune's effects we are still like the primitive or child who fears the dark. Many of the qualities belonging to Neptune are feared because we've been taught to fear whatever we can't put our finger on, whatever we can't control or pigeonhole. We've been taught daydreaming is a waste of time; hearing voices and seeing visions are insanity, "it's *only* imagination"; dreams are *only* dreams; logic is superior to intuition, etc. Fortunately for us the world's greatest composers and musicians, scientists, artists, inventors et al didn't pay too close attention to these admonitions. Without the dreamers, without the courage to explore the unknown, without the inspiration of Neptune, we'd live a sorely sterile existence. Neptune teaches us that isn't *all* there is.

THE NEPTUNE EFFECT comes for the most part from a series of lectures based on my personal experience of Neptune transiting my own chart, as well as those of my friends and clients. The majority of the work is based on first-hand experience, the rest on observation. The use of deductive reasoning is not altogether lacking in some instances and where it's used I say so.

I cannot stress enough the importance of the section "Psychological Orientation" in The Effect chapter. The reader is strongly advised to read it carefully before going on to the descriptions of Neptune's transits to the planets and other sensitive points. Some insight into an individual's psychological orientation is crucial to a proper and sane interpretation of the Neptune transit.

The Symbol

*I*n primitive thought, Neptune was the god of the Upper Waters, of clouds and rain. Later he became the god of fresh and fertilizing water. And finally he was known as the god of the sea. Cirlot, in *A Dictionary of Symbols*, says, "In this development we can trace not only a chronological and historical line of progress but, more especially, a spiritual projection of the myth of the 'fall,' which finally became absorbed into the character of Neptune...."*

The gods of legend and mythology came about as a result of the projection of qualities inherent within human nature. It's much easier to cope with things not readily understood when they are put outside the human sphere and put somewhere else, like Mt. Olympus. By putting, or projecting, these qualities outside they are then considered as not belonging to us but to someone or something else. The gods are responsible—we are the victims of their vagaries and whims.

Neptune undoubtedly has a relationship with the deepest layers of the individual and the universal soul (Jung's collective

*A Dictionary of Symbols, Philosophical Library, 1962, p. 217.

unconscious). Neptune is Lord of the Deeps. This is the planet of the power of the imagination which comes from the unconscious. As we know, imagination has its vagaries and whims and is not easily pigeonholed, therefore not readily understood.

Neptune is the archetypal ruler of the sea and all things liquid and, as such, represents aspects of the unconscious stirrings within us that are difficult to perceive or understand. The unconscious is full of vague "stuff." With his trident Neptune stirs up the sea and shatters rocks from which fountains spring forth. The myth tells us much about the power of Neptune, for on the inner level of the psyche the positive power of Neptune is to stir the depths of one's being, causing creative imagination to spring forth from the hard rock of ego consciousness. The ego is the rock which Neptune shatters. When rigid ego concepts are dissolved, our Neptune aspects surface. All our delusions swim before us and begin to dissolve, only to be replaced by new ones. Neptune calls forth from the sea the bulls and horses—the symbolic expression of the resurgence of cosmic energy from the primordial ocean. He rides the horses upon the waves, symbols of blind forces of primal chaos. He is the god of the unconscious and of sin; his realm is the haunt of monsters and baser forms of life. He rules over the monsters of the deep, of our souls. He is king of the deeps of the unconscious and of the turbulent waters of life; he unleashes storms, which symbolize the passions of the soul. He is also the subduer of storms.

Neptune's trident is identified with the magic wand. He is the Supreme Magician, the dealer of illusions. The trident, it should be noted, is also an attribute of Satan as well as Shiva, The Destroyer.

This is the powerful symbol of Neptune.

The Effect

*T*he exact aspect of transiting Neptune can be in effect for up to two years. However, the approaching aspect can be felt up to five years prior to the exact aspect. It must be borne in mind that while Neptune's aspect is in, other transiting aspects are simultaneously occurring. Therefore it's sometimes difficult to discern which effects belong to Neptune and which belong to the other transiting planets.

For example, Neptune transiting opposition to natal Uranus coincided with a marriage taking place, but everyone having this transit will not marry. In this particular case the First and Seventh houses were involved and transiting Jupiter was in exact conjunction to natal Uranus in the Seventh house at the time of the marriage. Neptune's part was evident in the fact that the owner of this chart was very confused (Neptune transiting the 1st) about the relationship which had been erratic (natal Uranus in the 7th) and didn't know what to do about it. She suddenly (Uranus) and inexplicably (Neptune) found herself married.

It's necessary to comprehend as well as possible the particular, if somewhat nebulous, character of Neptune. The house Neptune is transiting, the aspect(s) it makes, the planet(s) it aspects and the sign and house position of the aspected planet(s) must be taken into consideration to get an idea of the possibilities of Neptune's effect. Further, if you want more detail, all natal and transiting aspects made to the Neptune-aspected planet(s) should be taken into account. This can be a prodigious feat, especially if the chart is of the eclectic or splash variety. I recommend the simpler method: Neptune's house by transit, the planet(s) being aspected and its sign and house position. This will give a fair idea of the areas to be brought under Neptune's domination.

The Natal Position

Along with Uranus and Pluto, Neptune in the birth chart symbolizes the generation into which an individual is born. Because these planets are in one sign and can be in aspect to each other for such long periods, one or more of them must be in an Angular house or tied in by aspect with a personal planet: the Sun, Moon, Mercury, Venus, Mars, Jupiter or Saturn. However, if these generation planets make natal aspects only to Jupiter or Saturn they won't be as powerful in the chart unless they are also tied into the more personal planets. The more closely Neptune is tied in with the personal planets, the more its qualities will manifest in the person and his life. A natal trine or square of Nep-tune to Pluto strikes a dumb note in a chart unless it involves per-sonal planets. An individual with this square or trine tied into natal Mercury, however, will certainly be affected very personally by it; and transits to that configuration will be important in the life. Transits of the generation planets to an unaffecting natal con-figuration (Neptune square Pluto by itself for example) will be so subtle as to be almost meaningless. This is very important to keep in mind. We all know people who have horrific transits but nothing happens—inside or outside. They sail right though the transits as if nothing is happening and astrology doesn't work. This confounds many new students until they realize there has to be a personal connection for the transit to have an effect. I've also known people to have transiting Pluto conjunct their Ascendant, or transiting Uranus opposing their Sun. In both cases there were personal connections in the natal chart; but the changes took place almost entirely on an inner level. So don't always expect to be able to see a transit working externally.

As previously stated, Neptune is Lord of the Deeps, of the unconscious, of the universal soul. This puts it in charge of the very deepest layers of the collective psyche along with Jupiter, Saturn, Uranus and Pluto. We can't say that one planet rules the collective psyche simply because there are so many gradations within it. I agree with Jung when he says it's a mistake to try to separate and make finite the contents of the unconscious. It's a mistake, a trap, and impossible. The whole merges constantly, there are no clear boundary lines within the psyche. To try to pick it apart and define the various levels as separate from the rest would be like trying to define a human by looking at a nail clipping. In our finite way of thinking we would like to be able to compartmentalize and label things because this gives us the illusion of understanding the thing named. Unfortunately, or fortunately, existence defies such clear definitions as we would like to give it. So when I say Neptune is ruler of the deepest layers of the unconscious, I mean it is one of its aspects and, being a god of the waters, quite possibly one of the most primal.

Neptune is the power of the imagination. Sometimes we aren't prepared for Neptune's imaginings and think we have finally gone off the deep end when it approaches us. Neptune is the voice of the creative imagination. It isn't unusual for an individual with a natal or transiting contact of this planet to natal Mercury to hear voices—especially with the square aspect. It's imperative that this person tune into the voice rather than shut it off due to fear. It should be understood that this is the voice of inner creativity and it has something important to say.

Neptune is the Magician—it deals in illusions. Since it is the planet of illusion, it brings deceit and can be dangerous. It can align us with strange people and weird circumstances. It can move us to seek escape from the everyday world into alcohol, drugs or wanderlust. Neptune also gives inspiration. It can move us to reach for the unattainable so that we have that as an excuse for failure. It can also inspire us to reach for the heights of the nonmaterial world and reach a spirituality few attain. Or it can inspire us to reach for those heights and never return. It's the dreamer in us; the daydreamer or the one who brings his visions back to earth and gives them substance.

There's a certain vagueness about this planet and the "Neptunian type" emits this quality. You feel you aren't "connecting" with them; verbal communication with them is sometimes difficult and frustrating. Very often they are circumlocute in their conversation and can drive a linear-minded person up a wall. They don't know the technique of "putting it in a nutshell." There's a tendency to embellishment as well as a trailing off in conversation, so that you wait for what seems interminable lengths of time for them to conclude a sentence or thought. These people aren't really all here—they are "here" and "there" simultaneously.

Neptune represents all that appears weird, strange, romantic and marvelous in life. It's known as the higher octave of Venus (the planet of more earthly illusions). Neptune is unearthly beauty, like something from a strange and marvelous planet. As the higher octave of Venus which is the concept of love on a personal level, Neptune is the concept of Universal Love that reaches beyond the selfishness of Venus.

There's a certain perverseness in Neptune. We are moved to do things we later wonder over. We may start out saying one thing and find ourselves saying quite the contrary, having no control over it and no idea as to why we're pursuing it. The short story by Poe, *The Imp of the Perverse*, gives a wonderful illustration of this Neptunian quirk. Because of its perverse nature, Neptune is looked to for perversions in the chart. These can range from food addiction to drug addiction to sex addiction and all types of "perverse" appetites. What's perverse? It's deviating from the right, true or correct. Of course, "right, true, correct" are all relative and subjective terms: whatever is right, true or correct for one person is not necessarily so for another, and so on. We are perverse when we deviate from what is right, true or correct for ourselves. When we do something that is harmful to ourselves or other life forms, something not in our best overall interests, something over which we seem to have no control, then we are dealing with perversity.

Since Neptune is the planet of the imagination, we look to it for illusions and delusions. It's an indicator of mental breakdown. We also look to it for medically undiagnosable or difficult to diagnose diseases and problems. Neptune is the indicator of subtle leakages in the system. For example, what may seem to be anemia may be a subtle drain of the body's vital energy and won't show up on medical tests. Iron tonics may be of no avail because another course of treatment is needed—usually, a change in attitude. In its very negative form the planet has a vampirizing effect—there is an inexplicable loss of energy, vitality and interest in the surroundings. This may be due to the sensitizing influence of the planet; one becomes like a psychic sponge, picking up everything in the atmosphere, including positive and negative feelings and emotions from others. This obviously drains the body's energies. There is physical tension as a result of "protecting" oneself from these vibrations. And it's the tension that drains off physical energy.

Neptune Transiting

There are two main qualities of the Neptune transit:
1) Extraordinary sensitivity and intensification;
2) on the negative side, extraordinary debility.
It can also: drain, dissolve, becloud, befuddle, trick (not this, not that. . .), deceive, softly illumine, confuse, confound, enthrall, enveigle, withdraw, absorb, dissipate, infuse, inspire, distort, expand, contract, inflate, elate, spiritualize, depress, dramatize, romanticize, soften, elevate, descend. And last but not least, Neptune gives a distorted sense of proportion.

The transits of this planet aren't often given much attention since many of the old astrology sources describe it as being too subtle an influence and not easily seen or recognized. I have no argument with this description. However, it is this very subtlety that gives Neptune its tremendous power; it's got you before you know what's happened. It seduces and then drains the vitality, energy, and spirit. Neptune is associated with the figure of Satan: he is the tempter, the seducer; he casts before us illusions and clouds our judgment, and we willingly follow as in a trance the tempting seductions of the primal incubus. Neptune is a powerful transit. If you know what can happen, what can result, you've got a good chance of getting something of value from it.

People who are naturally sympathetic to Neptune are able to absorb the vibrations of Neptune's influence and resonate with them. In this case a Neptune transit adds rather than takes away. These people are able to derive inspiration from the environment, have a capacity for flowing with it creatively, for going with the natural ebb and flow of their energies. They too are sensitized by the influence, but sensitized can be negative or positive: if there's an empathetic response, it's positive; when the response is fear, there is debility.

With Neptune there is a diffused awareness, a diffused perception. It brings dissolution, but dissolution becomes diffusion. Neptune dissolves rigid concepts, it diffuses them so that a mediating principle can reorient them, bring them together in a new form.

Psychological Orientation

The effects of any transit are exaggerated if there's a rigidness of concept related to the planet being transited. With Neptune, a person oriented to a "rational" approach all his life will undoubtedly have a more difficult and exaggerated response to the transit than a person who is less focused in "reality" thinking. "Rational" and "reality" are, of course, relative terms.

To get some idea of how Neptune's transits will affect an individual, it's helpful to know the person's psychological orientation, their primary response to life. A "head" person is used to focused awareness; a "feeling" person is used to diffused awareness. The rational-mind person can't tolerate the diffusion of Neptune. So the thinking and the sensation (one who trusts only the five senses) types will experience Neptune one way, and the intuitive and the feeling types will experience it another way.

The orientation is shown by the predisposition of the sign the Sun is in and by the balance of the elements in the chart. I'll try to give some idea of the diagnosis, but it is of necessity general and will require work on the reader's part to put it together in individual cases.

In his book *The Psychological Types*, Jung describes four basic ways in which people respond to their environment. These are: Thinking, Feeling, Sensation, Intuition. He places each of these four types within one of two categories: introvert or extravert. The four types are further placed within the categories of rational or irrational, masculine or feminine; and they are also broken down into their natural oppositions: thinking and feeling are naturally opposed because both can't operate simultaneously; sensation and intuition oppose each other for the same reason.

There appears to be some controversy and confusion regarding the assignment of the astrological elements to Jungs's four function-types. Since the description of these types results in a breakdown of sixteen character types, it's little wonder there's confusion.

Because of the complexity of Jung's function-types, I've decided to dispense with them. Instead, I've decided to work with the elements and the signs as they manifest in their actions and behavior, not in their intent or idealized descriptions.

Earth and Air

These two elements are predisposed to what we may call "focused awareness." Earth functions primarily in the substantive world, concerned with sensate awareness (perception through the five physical senses), the form and structure of things being "reality." Air is predisposed to cerebration: thinking, analyzing, "logic," "reason," naming, calculating, delineating, categorizing, etc. All these things come under the heading of focused awareness.

In very general terms these two elements are concerned with things as they appear to be, and tend to see life in rather concrete terms. Quite naturally, most of us, no matter what element our Sun is in, function on these levels too. But, the Earth and Air elements function *primarily* on these levels; this is the way they respond to life initially. Earth *believes* in what it can perceive with its five senses; Air *believes* life can be analyzed and categorized: in a sense, both try to reason their way through life. Both are primarily concerned with things that can be either perceived through the five physical senses or through the analytic process. Anything that is beyond these five senses or that can't be fit into a neat, controllable category, is considered suspect.

Fire and Water

These two elements are predisposed to what may be termed "diffused awareness." Fire functions primarily in the world of imagination, ideals, and intensity of feeling. Fire people are intense people, especially on the inner level. Water functions primarily on an intuitive and emotional level. Both elements are tuned in to their feelings and emotional responses, and—perhaps most important in understanding the differences between them and the Earth/Air types—these types tend to lend a good deal of credence to these responses.

Fire tends to base its judgments on personal feeling response: How does a thing feel to me? Is it right, or is it wrong? And they base their judgments on how the situation or thing feels to them. Fire is aware of the feeling tone of the environment: Are people in a good mood or not? What would be the appropriate response to this situation? (Whereas, for example, Air would tell it like it is without consideration of how it might affect the feelings of those around it.)

Water responds to feeling also; but it is primarily a "hunch" element and tends to go along with these hunches, or intuitions—no matter how illogical they may appear to the rest of the world. These are the dreamers, the mystics, the visionaries who are very much concerned with their own inner images. (Earth tends to see this type as very impractical and useless.)

Both Fire and Water do not generally focus on the details of a situation: they perceive things in context; that is, there is a general overview perceived, things are perceived in relationship; there is an awareness of the way things affect each other; there is no true black or white—they deal with "shadings." All this comes under the heading of diffused awareness.

Fire and Water are also concerned with reality as it appears to be, but that reality is quite different from the reality of Air and Earth. Fire and Water don't see things in such concrete terms—for them, there's always "more than meets the eye."

Ψ

Because of their differences in perception and response, these elements will experience Neptune differently. The element the Sun is in shows the predisposition of the person; but the balance of the elements will indicate the overall response given to life.

For example, Fire Sun (feeling) with a preponderance of Air and/or Earth planets in the natal chart won't respond as easily to a Neptune transit as Fire Sun with a preponderance of Fire/Water. The more Fire/Water in a chart the easier the response. The key word is "easy," which doesn't signify better or worse. It just means easier. Fire Sun with nothing but Fire/Water in the chart may be swept away by the Neptune influence; it has no "ground." A little Earth and/or Air is necessary to balance out the overall response. Earth is needed to keep the feet on the ground somewhat, and Air helps to give a "thoughtful" response to the experience. One or two, but no more, planets in Air, and one or two planets in Earth will do fine. On the other hand, three Earth and no Air won't do too badly! The problem with this, however, is that no Air tends to overcompensate: the individual tries to think out everything, and this is impossible with Neptune. Conversely, a person with three or more planets in Air is already confused about things in general and Neptune isn't going to help matters. Air lives too much on the cerebral level and not in the intuitive, feeling realm. Earth lives too much in the substantive world; it trusts only what it can perceive with its five senses. Anything else is suspect and sometimes feared. The more a person is predisposed to respond to life on a "rational" level, the more difficult the Neptune effect. These people aren't geared to flowing with circumstances; they tend to be controllers and manipulators of their environments; they are rooted in a substantive reality and don't easily tolerate or cope with the transitory nature of things.

This is, of course, very general; it is to be used merely as a guideline and is not meant in any way to be dogmatic. Trying to pin down someone as to which type he or she is, is further complicated by the fact that many people don't function according to their predisposition. That is, a person whose innate superior function is intuition but, because of environmental and cultural conditioning, has devalued that dominant function and has tried to operate with an innately "inferior" function, is out of kilter with himself. An intuitive type, for example, can appear to be an earthy, sensate type or an airy, thinking type if he was taught to believe that was what would get him ahead in the world. We can't neglect the fact that in our Western culture the functions of feeling and intuition as well as introversion have been devalued in general. And so we have a lot of people out of kilter with themselves. The chart of "X" will serve to illustrate this.

This horoscope is a good example of a naturally intuitive Sun (Pisces) overcome by a too-rigid, practical and materialistic approach to life (7 Fixed planets; 5 Earth and 3 Air).

In July 1968, "X" experienced his first psychotic episode in the form of a deep depression bordering on a "vegetative" state (extreme apathy) with which he could not cope as transiting Neptune was forming an opposition to the natal Moon-Uranus conjunction. The catalyst was the sudden and violent death of a younger brother whom he loved. [Transiting Uranus was forming a conjunction with natal Neptune, ruler of the Third house.] This was a great emotional loss.(See *Neptune Transiting Moon* section.)

As transiting Neptune continued on its journey to square his Sun, "X" began experiencing manic-depressive states over which he had no control. Shortly thereafter, Saturn made its first return August 1970.

During the two- to three-year period of Neptune's approach to his Ascendant, the manic-depressive states became intensified; he was in a constant state of flux between euphoria, ego inflation and delusions of grandeur and paralyzing depressions. At this time he began exhibiting extreme paranoic behavior: he distrusted everyone including long-time friends and his family; he was convinced the local state troopers were "out to get him"; that the FBI was spying on him; that underworld figures were trying to get him to transport drugs (Neptune!) into the country; and he carried a weapon for self-protection.

In August 1977 Saturn squared itself; during the first week of December 1977 as transiting Neptune approached 2° away from its first contact with his Ascendant, "X" had a nervous breakdown, *which he could recognize as such*, and sought psychiatric help for the first time. During the week of the breakdown the other transits were: transiting Saturn applying a square to his natal Sun, transiting Uranus in a 1° separating

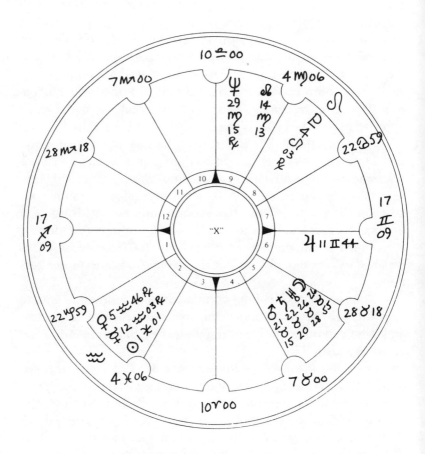

FIRE   1
EARTH 5
AIR   3
WATER 1

square from natal Mercury, and transiting Mars 1° applying opposition to natal Mercury.

As Neptune hovered over the Ascendant in 1978, "X" decided to commit himself to a psychiatric hospital for observation. He is currently an outpatient and has been stabilized with drug therapy (Lithium). Neptune isn't yet finished with his Ascendant and at this writing transiting Uranus is about to make its opposition to the Fifth house stellium and proceeds to square his Sun shortly thereafter.

During the period beginning with Neptune's opposition to his natal Moon-Uranus conjunction to the time of the crossing of his Ascendant, "X" married, fathered a child and was divorced a few years later by his wife. He was unable to continue in his profession as a pilot (he bagan to fear flying) and held various factory-type jobs during the interim. He bought and then sold at a loss a very expensive home; with credit cards charged a great deal of electronic equipment and other merchandise; had his credit revoked; got very drunk very often; was arrested many times for driving while intoxicated and sentenced to several weekends in jail. During this period he also: walked into a revolving helicopter blade, crashed in a light plane and walked away; and had several serious automobile accidents. He received no injuries from any of these except a small scar on his cheek from the helicopter blade. It's quite possible he has somehow *survived* all this because of the grand trine formed by natal Neptune to Venus and the Fifth house stellium! Those of you who have the heart for it are invited to check the transits of Jupiter, Saturn, Uranus and Pluto to "X's" chart for the period just described. It isn't within the scope of this small book to go into them.

"X" is a classic example of the type of stressful reactions that can result when there isn't sufficient flexibility in the chart and in the character of the individual. Obviously, a grand trine is of some benefit!

Ψ

If the Neptune transit is to be "successful" rather than totally debilitating, one or two planets in Earth/Air will be helpful; any more will tip the balance. All Fire/Water is too unstable; it needs Earth for stability and Air to reason.

A word should be mentioned about the Fixed signs since these people seem to have the most difficulty coping with transitoriness. Of the Fixed, Leo (Fire) and Scorpio (Water) will have slightly less difficulty than Aquarius (Air) and Taurus (Earth). But these two Fire and Water signs don't have the ease of the other Fire and Water signs.

The age and life experience of the person having a Neptune transit are also important factors in the diagnosis. The younger, the more immature and the less life experienced, the more difficult the transit. Also, the life-cycle must be considered: is the person experiencing a Saturn return, or a Uranus opposing Uranus, etc., during the Neptune transit? All these things must be taken into consideration.

It must also be pointed out that *any* aspect of Neptune transiting a sensitive point in the chart is sensitizing for better or worse. Even the "wonderful" trine can drain or dissipate, depending on the predisposition of the person. Possibly the sextile is the least hazardous of all.

♆

In the Preface I suggested that we aren't victims, much as some of us prefer to think of ourselves as such. Afterall, this puts the responsibility elsewhere, and the planets, like the government, are supposed to be in charge of things.

If it's true that we create our own conditions by our response to circumstances, then Neptune can't be considered the "reason" for the outcome. Nor can a transit of any planet. Neptune is known as a drainer, a debilitator; however, I suggest that it isn't Neptune that brings about this condition but the response given to its influence. If a person continually battles the Neptune influence with logic and reason and rigidity, that person will be very tired indeed and will feel a need for more rest than usual. If a person's response to its influence is one of fear, this can also be quite debilitating.

The science fiction/fantasy writer, H. P. Lovecraft, is a good example of the Neptunian type and of the debilitating response to the Neptune influence. Lovecraft's element breakdown is interesting in light of what is discussed above: 2 F, 2 E, 6 A, O W. He was a feeling type, but his Fixed Leo Sun

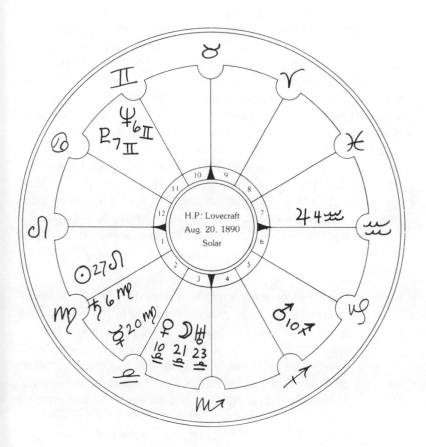

*Birth date obtained from "Lovecraft, A Biography," by L. Sprague De Camp, Ballantine Books, NY, 1976.

and his Virgo Mercury gave him a rigid and analytical approach to life, while his Libran Moon conjunct Uranus gave him no "ground" in his feelings. The Moon-Uranus conjunction also made him hypersensitive and "a nervous wreck," as he so aptly described himself. HPL was what we would define as a "head" person, a man who engaged in a good deal of cerebration and for all practical purposes was out of touch with his feeling/emotional side. His chart also contains what I call the "aspect of fear": Pluto conjunct Neptune square Sun conjunct Saturn. (Neptune square Saturn gives unreasoning, irrational fears; HPL worried a good deal about his sanity.) To make this aspect of fear even stronger, it's tied into a T-square with Mars opposing the Pluto-Neptune conjunction. HPL was also physically debilitated most of his short life. Lovecraft's stories vividly illustrate the fearful and truly weird imagination the man possessed. In Lovecraft we find genius suffocated by fear. The following will give some idea of the magnitude of his fearfulness, especially regarding the world within:

> The most merciful thing in the world, I think, is the inability of the human mind to correlate all its contents. We live on a placid island of ignorance in the midst of black seas of infinity, and it was not meant that we should voyage far. . . . but some day the piecing together of dissociated knowledge will open up such terrifying vistas of reality, and of our frightful position therein, that we shall either go mad from the revelation or flee from the deadly light into the peace and safety of a new dark age. *

This opening paragraph of Lovecraft's story about an ancient god of the primordial abyss who lies in wait beneath the earth's waters until "the stars are right" for him to rise, refers to knowledge contained within the collective unconscious. HPL's fearful imagination saw only madness or a flight to ignorance as the end result of seeing those "vistas of reality" and "our frightful position therein." But there is another alternative: freedom from the protective coverlet of material illusion. Madness, "blissful" ignorance, or revelation: one of these is the final destination of the voyage with Neptune.

*The Dunwich Horror and Others, "The Call of Cthulhu," Arkham House, 1963, p. 130.

Although Neptune brings us into contact with the unknown, we must never think for a moment Neptune is outside ourselves: we must never forget Neptune is us and we are it. By consciously following the Lord of the Deeps to his primigenial lair we may discover a light that will forever make us free of illusion.

The Transit

*T*he Neptune quality of dissolution works upon and effects a transformation of the qualities of the planet it touches. Specific aspects are not given; the transits are defined in terms of "stressful" and "nonstressful" contacts. For example, a conjunction of Neptune to a sensitive point in the chart will be stressful for one type of individual and quite the contrary for another type (see *Psychological Orientation*, p. 23). The transit descriptions are meant to give as broad an idea as possible of Neptune's potential.

The following descriptions of Neptune's transits to the natal planets also apply in large part to the aspects of natal Neptune to the natal planets. That is, someone born with natal Neptune in stressful aspect to the Sun will respond similarly to the person experiencing Neptune's stressful transit to their natal Sun. There does seem to be one difference however: individuals with the natal aspect are familiar with it! They've lived with it all their lives and have learned to deal with it in their own way. The vibrations of Neptune aren't as alien to them, whereas individuals experiencing Neptune's contact to their Sun for the first time are thrown off-guard. For some people with natal aspects of Neptune

to Mercury, for example, hearing voices, hearing one's name called and finding no one in sight, are not uncommon. Some have
learned to live with it, some remain apprehensive of it (due to
mis-education) and some think it's "slightly crazy" but. . . so
what? Isn't *everyone* a little crazy? Besides, people who are a "little crazy" are far more interesting and creative than so-called
"normal" people. But picture the person experiencing transiting
Neptune's effect for the first time on his Mercury. Suddenly hearing voices can be a little unsettling to say the least.

So this is the difference between a natal Neptune contact
and a transiting Neptune contact. They both have much in common but one has been experienced since birth and the other is a
brand-new experience. Obviously the transit is more difficult to
manage — until one gets the hang of it.

Sun

The Sun represents the vitality and essence of the person;
this is the symbol of ego consciousness, the sense of "I am."
Some of what is said about Neptune transiting the Sun may be
applied to Neptune transiting the Ascendant.

When Neptune contacts the natal Sun by transit the person becomes infused with the Neptunian qualities. Often, the person is thought to be a Piscean, especially with the conjunction.
The Neptune effect here is extremely sensitizing and creates a
"psychic sponge." As a result of this there can be a sense of low
vitality, a lack of energy that may make you suspect you have
some strange, exotic disease. Psychosomatic illnesses can arise
or things not easily diagnosable. At the very least you may suspect you're anemic, but a blood test will show that you're as
healthy as the proverbial horse. Vitamins and cell salts* are helpful if this condition arises, as well as the knowledge of what transit
you're under and a concomittant change of attitude and response.

Sleep beckons and can become an obsession but it is often
unrestful; the body and mind feel tired to the core, but insommia
often occurs. This can be a wretched state because there is no
deep rest and no energy to get up from bed to do something constructive. You can't sleep, you can't work. Inertia can become

*a homeopathic remedy.

overwhelming and result in guilt feelings because you feel you
should be *doing* something. A sort of limbo sets in—you feel you
are nowhere, suspended in a void, no up, no down. This can be
very disconcerting. But gradually even that feeling vanishes and
there is no response to anything. Apathy sets in. You may fall into periods of "vegetation." Suicide is dispassionately considered;
death is the ultimate escape from this level of earthly existence. It
seems the only sensible thing to do since there is obviously no
reason to remain here. So, the feeling is "why not go on to
whatever is next, or end it completely, if that's the case?" The
danger with this state is that the suicide can be "successful"
because the person isn't feeling anything—no anger, no depression, nothing. And they tend to seek solitude because of a feeling
of disconnectedness with their surroundings. They do need time
alone; it's necessary to their survival at this time because they are
oversensitve to their environment and become easily sapped of
energy. Counseling at this time can be invaluable because these
people feel "lost."

     When the inertia or apathy state sets in, this is the clue that
all the vital energy or libido is submerged in the unconscious. That
energy is not available to the conscious person and this is why
they feel "lost" and sometimes useless and powerless. Because
the energy is submerged, they can also sometimes look anemic or
half-alive. They do feel as if only one of their eight cylinders are
functioning! Since the libido has taken a plunge into the unconscious, this is where "the work" is going on and why it's so difficult to engage in mundane industry. It takes enormous effort at
times just to maintain consciousness; imagine the effort it must
take to do anything strenuous. Lovecraft states in his biography
that it took enormous energy for him just to walk from his bed to a
nearby chair.

     When the energy is released from the unconscious (which
can take months), a manic state often accompanies it. The lower
the "low," the higher the "high." It can be difficult to maintain a
personality equilibrium during this transit. This is why counseling
can prove beneficial. It helps to maintain some semblance of
perspective, and one can more effectively work with the contents
rising to the conscious level. One wonders what all that weird stuff
is and feels better if it can be discussed with someone who has

some understanding of unconscious processes and who isn't going to be judgemental.

Because they are extraordinarily sensitive to the environment, individuals with a transiting Neptune soak up everything around them. They are very aware in a diffused way of everything surrounding them. And their feelings are easily hurt. Their moods are not always their own for they can pick up the moods and feelings of others and have difficulty separating their own from those of others. There is psychic attunement, an ability to "read" others, to feel them.

This can be a time of great love, either for someone or the world in general; it can work both ways simultaneously. The inspiration side of Neptune stimulates the creative element of the nature; artists who have been in fallow periods are suddenly able to create again because the muse has once more returned.

There can be strong fears, irrational and imaginary. The imagination becomes stronger, vivid dreams and nightmares occur, and the psychic/fantasy life becomes activated. Writing out dreams and fantasies is a good outlet, a way of channeling the energy, of giving it its due.

Since the Sun is ego consciousness, there can occur identity problems, a feeling of not being yourself: who am I? what am I? This is a highly confusing period. Sometimes the person wants to spend lots of time alone due to the increased sensitivity to the environment; this can be a period of introversion because it becomes increasingly difficult to relate to others.

Alcohol, drugs or gambling may be used as a means of escape. These things can be highly dangerous under this transit because the Sun is embroiled in delusions and illusions.

Once you settle into the transit and stop fighting it and learn to flow with it, revelations and personal and spiritual insights are gained. The insights can be so overwhelming that you want to run into the streets and tell everyone. But you quickly learn that not only are words inadequate but people can't understand *your* experience. You also begin to realize they're looking at you a little oddly and you may decide it's smarter to keep your mouth shut before they ship you off to the funny farm. It's important for you to realize this is *your* experience; you can't share it, try as you may. You soon figure this out: it doesn't matter if you share it because *you've* learned something important, *you* understand it, and that's all that truly matters. You may also realize that people will have to experience it for themselves, you can't give it to them; and then let go of your messiah complex.

There is usually a loss of some sort when Neptune contacts the Sun. Sometimes the father is affected in some way. Or it can work on an inner level: you become alienated in your experience and in the knowledge you're deriving from it because you can't communicate it to others. This is a dangerous period because it's easy to slip into this feeling of alienation or a "God complex" and stay there. You can lose the world. The mystics throughout the ages have said the initiate, once becoming illumined, must return to the world. He can't stay on the mountaintop. You can't stay there because on the mountain you become totally merged with the Infinite. By staying there you remain merged. In analytical psychology this is known as identifying with the contents of the collective unconscious. When we touch the ineffable we must know our connection to IT but we must also know *we are not IT*. If identification becomes total, death of the ego personality takes place and unconsciousness ensues. The end result is easily seen in those whom we refer to as insane.

So this is a transit that can take you very far out, but you have to come back under your own power. Neptune entices and seduces but if you recognize it, it can't hold power over you. It's crucial for you to maintain an awareness of your physical self while you're experiencing your infinite Self. That is, it's crucial if you wish to return. There's a choice. The fundamental experience of this effect is knowing Infinity, and the experience of this knowing can literally blow your mind away.

There are those who mentally (perhaps psychically) travel into the universe. There can be a sense of reaching what can only be described as the edge of infinity. There may be at this time vivid dreams of outer space, other worlds and cultures, space travel, space ships and encounters with those from other worlds. There may be dreams of flying or floating with no vehicle but the body. There may be out-of-body experiences.

There is a feeling at times as if the whole person, the entire being is disintegrating, physically crumbling. This can be a terrifying experience unless you have some understanding of what is happening: the ego personality is undergoing a profound change, your self-concepts and concepts of everything around you are changing, transforming. If you understand that a disintegration process is necessary for the restructuring of the personality, it will make the experience less frightening, although nevertheless uncomfortable!

There can be indescribable moments of ecstacy as well as agony. The person becomes "spiritualized," infused with the Neptunian energy, and of course this can go in many directions and to extremes. But for a person of some maturity (age has nothing to do with it) this can be an extraordinarily life-enhancing transit, one of a lifetime. Anyone who has experienced this transit will tell you they wouldn't have missed it for the world, even though extremes of agony and suffering had to be endured in order for a reorientation of personality to take place. They will also almost certainly tell you once was enough!

In a chart where the Sun is badly afflicted there is the possibility of catatonic states, narcolepsy, or coma. It would be especially interesting to research cases of people going into comatose states for a while and then suddenly coming out. Such research can be vital in lieu of the fact that society is becoming more reasonable regarding "pulling the plug." I'd hate to have someone pull my plug when Neptune is on me.

The possible final outcome of Neptune to the Sun, especially with the conjunction, is a definite knowledge of the connection of all things. It is no longer an intellectual concept. Through the terrifying isolation of the transit comes an understanding of the interconnectedness of all life and that the only thing that separates or alienates us is our intellect. We are alone in our heads. And that is the most agonizing alienation. Neptune teaches you to feel in the truest sense of the word, and for one not used to feeling, the effect at first can be devastating because the agony is so extreme. The skin of the body can become painful to touch, even to the touch of air. Although Neptune is a water deity, the transit brings us to the burning ground and there we are set on fire to be destroyed or purified.

Moon

The Moon represents the emotional responses, deep feelings, the protective, nurturing response, responsiveness in general, and the body's functioning, as well as the mother and women very close to you.

Tragic love affairs seem to be common when Neptune touches the natal Moon; there are sometimes great emotional losses. Some lose the lover during or after this transit. So it seems to indicate a loss which strongly affects the emotions.

Emotions and feelings are strongly sensitized. There can be an overwhelming urge to self-sacrifice in the name of love. Emotional trauma can take place regarding love where a person may vow never to love again. Marry under this transit and when it pulls out you may find the honeymoon is definitely over.

The emotional life is tremendously affected; there can be fear of expressing the emotions, feelings and sexual needs. There may be insecurity and a good deal of crying. Sometimes tears suddenly begin flowing for no apparent reason. A sense of not knowing what to do with the life drives some to seek identity. This seems to be especially the case with women. Women close to you at this time may present emotional difficulties; they may themselves experience emotional problems, perhaps nervous breakdown. There may be confusion, fears and anxieties regarding them, and in the homelife as well.

The body's functions can be affected: weight loss or gain seems to be common. Young women approaching puberty may experience "strange" menses; menstruation may begin early and suddenly stop and return a couple of years later. Women in the menopause cycle may also experience "strange" conditions. The female biological cycles may be more confusing to women undergoing a transit of Neptune to their Moon. Nervous disorders may occur, either your own or someonce close to you. People have been known to go onto tranquilizers *after* this transit. Apparently the emotional sensitivity and consequent strain grows and grows during the transit, and when Neptune releases its energy the emotional tensions are also released. Nervous breakdown has occured in some cases after the transit.

Confusing circumstances surrounding the mother, wife, or

a woman close to you can crop up. There can be emotional drains in the life; misplaced sympathies and feelings, emotional responses are out of proportion to the situation. Some person or persons in the life pull on your emotions and you may feel torn apart.

There can be an increased flair for the dramatic when it comes to emotional responses and expression, overresponding to situations and people. There can arise a need to be seen as a victim, feelings of self-pity, seeing yourself in the role of "Camille." There's a strong need for sympathy from others and you'll display your emotions in order to get it.

There is the chance with Neptune to transform the emotional nature, to bring it up out of selfishness and put it on a level that can be realistically helpful to others, where your emotional responses are real rather than feigned or coming from selfish motivations. Overreacting to another's dilemma doesn't help them.

The nurturing instinct can become sensitized; you want to take care of some poor soul. You also want someone to take care of you. The biological urge is also stimulated, a need to create a child for all the wrong reasons. There may be an unrealistic and romantic ideal surrounding mothering and parenting that has nothing to do with the everyday reality of childbearing and childrearing. Neptune makes it easy to get caught up in the romance of having babies. This is a time for the body's misuse and abuse by oneself or others.

You become susceptible to the vibrations in the home atmosphere. There may be sorrow and great sadness in the home or pertaining to domestic matters. Disappointments may also result in these areas. Things may not be what they seem to be.

Intuition may become heightened, so hunches often prove to be correct. Follow them but be sure to also investigate them. You "feel" things more intensely with a Neptune contact to your Moon and if you're the type of person who's poo-poo'd intuition, now's the time to check it out. You may learn to trust it for the first time in your rational life. A nice present from Neptune.

Wherever the Moon is placed in the chart and wherever Neptune is transiting, these will be the areas of oversensitivity and this will be where you are most vulnerable and easily sapped and suckered in.

Mercury

This planet symbolizes the mind, thought processes and ability to communicate: in general, the mental functions. This transit has some similar effects of the Sun-Neptune transit.

Neptune touching natal Mercury brings in confusion. It's a "worrying" transit. You worry particularly about your sanity. People who don't drink alcohol may find themselves suddenly keeping it in the cupboard. At first there may be some anxiety as to whether or not one is becoming an alcoholic. However, if one is aware of the transit in effect, the worry and anxiety will be lessened. Those who have been occasional or social drinkers may find their drinking increased and tend to worry about it.

Bouts of uncontrollable shivering or shuddering occasionally occur which can be embarrassing because you can't stop it. This happens when your nervous system is overstimulated. Since it usually happens when you're around someone or other people, go to a room where you can be alone until it passes, and if possible listen to soothing music.

There are unpleasant periods of confusion, mental lapses, and a lot of anxiety in general. It is in fact a period difficult to recall when it's over! This is one reason to keep a diary, journal or notebook so you can look back and see what happened. The mind can become clouded; there may be no energy or desire to communicate, or intense difficulty in communication. A period of introversion sets in as a result. As with the Sun, there can be a good deal of sleeping but with no real rest. Again, insomnia is an effect. The quality of sleep may improve when you begin working with the influence rather than fighting it.

There can be so much confusion that you may not know what to do with your life and feel a need to pull your "head" together. There is often so much difficulty in making decisions that others may run your life for you during this transit.

Travel can be confounding even in familiar circumstances. You may find yourself on your way to someplace you've been a thousand times and suddenly forget where it was you were headed or how to get there. It can be difficult to hold thoughts, and concentration is almost nonexistant. Concentration can be so poor that you may think you've suddenly become a very stupid person. Grasping anything of a technical nature or trying to learn something new can at times be a most difficult and frustrating experience. You can become exasperated at your inability to retain *anything*. Memories can be so vague you can't remember if something actually happened or if you dreamed it. So there's confusion regarding dream and awake states. They sometimes seem to merge. One of the most mystifying things of this transit is that you think you've told someone something when you've only thought the thought. You then wonder why *they* forgot. Naturally, this brings about misunderstandings and you begin to doubt your intelligence and ability to communicate. You also tend to forget things told to you and when you're reminded of your negligence you swear up and down you were never told anything of the sort! You were undoubtedly told; you just weren't paying attention at the time because there was some Neptunian thing preoccupying your mind and you nodded absently at the person just to get rid of them.

Frightening dreams and nightmares may occur. Your dreamlife may become of increasing interest since dream activity is stimulated by this transit. Psychic studies and such things as working with the ouija board and automatic writing become fascinating; utter absorption with psychic phenomena can occur. The danger is that the interest may grow so great that it turns into an obsession. If you begin to question these things rather than becoming enthralled by them, insights can be gained through heightened mental and intuitive perceptions.

Because of a sense of isolation brought about by difficulty in communicating there may come the realization that no one can help you but yourself. Through this experience of *aloneness* you begin to realize that it is communication in its narrow sense that has been alienating you so completely from others. Once this is understood it's one short step to an awareness of your connection with everyone and everything. Your concepts of communication become reoriented. There is an ability to pick up vibes and understand them. There can be successful telepathic attempts; you may call a person mentally and find them responding physically. You may also learn the truth of the old adage "be careful of what you want. . ." because you may find with this transit you get it.

There may occur an awareness of the other sides of the personality within. Sometimes inner dialogue with these other facets of yourself takes place. At times "voices" are distinctly heard. Or music is heard clearly and distinctly even though there's no tangible source.

Sense perceptions are heightened. There may be very vivid mental-feeling memories, flashbacks wherein all five senses are operating. There may also be a slipping or splitting feeling in the head, as if you're about to slip into another dimension. This can be a very definite physical sensation, as if a gear had shifted. There can be split-second flashes of memories, intensely felt, unidentifiable and timeless. All these things occur in a natural state.

There may be indulgences in romantic reveries, lots of daydreaming, mental travel and so on. The fantasy life is often increased, and writing is suggested as an outlet because the imagination is strong and can be very, very vivid. It all needs channeling.

With a stressful contact of Neptune to Mercury, deep depressions are a common feature of this transit. There is a good deal of ruminating taking place; the individual is ingesting information coming both from the inner and the outer spheres of experience. It's a period of assimilation and gestation. As a consequence of this activity, the psychic energies are "stuck" in the deeper levels of the unconscious where they are needed for the processing of the information. Since the energy isn't at hand to do the bidding of the conscious mind the person is left feeling powerless, impotent, and depression results. Suicidal thoughts are also not uncommon, especially with those who have considered such action before. The more introspective, sensitive types are no strangers to the idea of suicide. In fact, for many the idea of suicide is part and parcel of their existence.

The only thing to do when such deep depressions set in is to flow *with* the depression. Fighting it only makes matters worse. Try to be still, be quiet with the depressive mood and see what you can discover about it. Sometimes nothing will present itself to consciousness; at other times material will come up. Very often there's a tendency to fight the depressive mood until, finally, you feel like you've reached the end of your rope and you simply give up. Fighting it creates constant frustration and anger. When you give up, creative energies have a chance to begin to surface. For example, during one of her Neptune depressions a client gave up after trying to apply her meager energies to her work and found herself creating hand-made birthday cards for her friends and writing very witty letters with cartoons in the margin. What she did was not of a prize-winning quality. What *is* important is that she felt much better mood-wise because part of her creativity had been given expression.

Listening to soothing or classical music can be of tremendous value. Neptune rules stringed instruments and when you listen to a lovely violin concerto it's almost like you're giving Neptune his due. Time and time again my personal experience has shown me that depressions have their reason. If we'll just be quiet and listen to them we'll discover the reason. We won't always like what we discover; but as long as that reason remains unconscious it has control over us, like it or not. The discovery of it is the first step in the natural healing process of the mind.

Venus

This planet signifies one's fundamental values and desires, as well as the concept of femininity and the expression of affection.

The transit of Neptune to natal Venus brings confusion and delusion regarding love matters and friendships in general. This transit can bring the fantasy or dream lover. There can be illicit or numerous love affairs as well as promiscuity due to a fear of losing sexual attraction or attractiveness.

Men with this transit find themselves in relationships with the strangest women. It brings into the life people who are "different" from those you've been dealing with up to this time.

There may be intense confusion regarding what you want in life in terms of the things you wish to possess—animate and inanimate. You may question your values or concepts of what is valuable and meaningful in life. There may be deception and delusions and deviousness in friendships and social matters. You may not know who is really your friend or you may trust someone who is unworthy. Women with this transit feel an uncertainty about their femininity or attractiveness. There can be some confusion regarding what being a "woman" is all about. There is also confusion in giving love and affection; it's usually given to the "wrong" person or out of pity. Because of the uncertainty revolving around one's appeal, promiscuity may occur; this is a means of proving that you are still attractive or of proving to yourself that you really are attractive. There is also the possibility that Neptune may take away the desire for sex or romantic involvement, and this may result in compensatory activity such as promiscuity to prove to yourself that everything's o.k. (See *Mars* for further amplification of the compensatory function.)

There can occur an overindulgence of the love nature. A Jupiter-like expansion can take place; going after the "good things of life" to the point where it becomes debilitating. Moderation is an unknown at this time! Friendships with "different" or "strange" types are made, and when the transit of Neptune ends so may the friendships because you are able to better judge them later.

Laziness and a love of ostentatious luxury may occur. A "put off until tomorrow" attitude may prevail.

The concept of "love" is clouded—what is it? There may be extremes experienced in this area. Love may become such an ideal that it can never be realized. A love of things "Neptunian" may come about—that is, all things connected with Neptune become enthralling. One's sense of drama and art is heightened so that this can be a highly productive period in terms of creativity for those of an artistic leaning or occupation. The theater and arts of all types become like magnets. There can be a tightening of the net of illusion regarding beauty. One may suddenly decide that one wants to be on the stage; if that isn't possible, the personal life will take on a tone of drama.

The illusion of beauty may be broken under this transit if it's worked with. Neptune won't allow you to stay on the surface of things for long if you follow it.

Very romantic love affairs are desired and one is sucked in by the very idea. Stories of such affairs are enchanting during this transit and one's sympathies are in accord with anyone "suffering" the pangs of love.

There can be losses in terms of loved ones or objects. A much-loved vase or a love affair may be broken. In such cases there is intense suffering over the loss, perhaps accompanied by a bit of exaggeration and dramatization. There can be a desire to be seen as a tragic victim of love. You want to be sacrificed on the altar of love. You may set yourself up as a victim in love matters in order to accomplish your goal of martyrdom.

There can be "gushiness" with this transit: oversentimental expressions of or a need for affection; overemphasizing Venusian qualities such as overdressing and lavish "productions" of all sorts. (I think the great Busby Berkeley of Hollywood must have had a Neptune-Jupiter-Venus conjunction!)

However, with a less stressful aspect a sensitive touch may be developed and applied to areas formerly lacking a proper feeling response. Relationships can be enhanced because your response in your friendships is more sensitive and feeling. There may be empathy with "feminine" values and concepts when this may have been previously lacking. The same holds true for Neptune touching the Moon. In both cases the feelings are more responsive and empathetic. One's sympathies are aroused.

With any contact of Neptune to Venus, all Venusian concepts may become dissolved and reoriented to a more universal level. They are taken from the personal level of selfishness and uplifted to the universal. When this occurs with a stressful contact it's more painful in arriving. Buddha said life is truly sorrowful; but Venus can't see the true sorrow because of the illusion of sorrow. When the truth of the Buddha proclamation is perceived, then and only then can the true beauty of life be recognized and held precious.

Mars

Mars represents the physical energies and sexual function and concepts, as well as one's ability to take action.

When Neptune touches natal Mars, especially the square aspect, there may occur a loss of sexual energy or a loss of desire for sex. There may be no sexual activity or very little while the influence is in effect. In the case of the opposition, sexual desire may be present but the opportunities for expression aren't or are not readily available. This can be a very interesting transit if you're inclined to observation for, being eliminated from the race, you have the opportunity to sit back and watch with some objectivity, and no little amusement. The possible end result of such observation can be a reorienting of your own sexual needs. You have the opportunity to find out what it is *you* need sexually as opposed to what you *thought* you needed. Your priorities get shifted. A fundamental change of sexual attitudes can come about as a result of this transit.

If there is a loss of sex drive it can be excruciating at first, especially if you're married or involved in a sexual relationship. At first you think there's something dreadfully wrong with you; then you begin to think your partner is oversexed. Seeing a doctor regarding your debility is usually of no help; even taking "sex boosters" or hormone treatment has been known to be ineffective. It just isn't there. The only thing you can do under such circumstances is to relax and try to get your partner to relax. It's a temporary phenomenon. Once you relax you'll both begin to get some insights into the matter of sex. However, before these insights come in, the situation can be hellish.

Sometimes there is no loss of sex drive; in fact, it appears to be increased. Again, Neptune has a bit of Jupiter in it—overdoing, inflation, overindulgence, and so on. There is the possibility that when the sexual activity is increased rather than decreased, the increased desire is the result of a feeling of a loss of desire. That is, compensation sets in. If you're used to being sexually active and begin to find it lagging you're going to go about rectifying the matter—even if it takes every ounce of willpower and energy. This is how "Neptune" drains. Because there are feelings of impotence, there is an attempt to contradict what you're feeling so that you go overboard to prove to yourself and everyone else that everything's o.k. So with this transit, misuse and abuse of the energies can take place: plain old sex becomes boring and/or ineffective; overindulgence in sexual matters; dissipation through sex; seeking the different and strange in sex partners and activities. A sense of proportion is lacking.

Sexuality may be transformed; it can become "spiritualized" and a more sensitive response is given in lovemaking. It can become so "spiritualized" that it's given up and entirely rechanneled. Just be certain it isn't being repressed. One may feel such "animality" isn't "spiritual," therefore giving up sex for the wrong reason. On the other hand, energy formerly channeled into sexual activity may become channeled into other areas so that sex is entirely "forgotten" during the transit. It's a matter of a shift of priorities in this case. This is especially likely if one is involved in some creative aspect of the life, where the energies are totally channeled into the nonmaterial or spiritual or creative pursuits. It must be borne in mind that sexual energy is fundamentally creative energy; when an individual is establishing some creative aspect of himself this energy is no longer necessarily sexual. But because it's no longer sexual this doesn't mean the person will never be sexual again. This is a transitory phenomenon; the energy is simply needed elsewhere.

In the case of a woman who up to the time of this transit has "lived her life for her man," she may find her sexual needs very gradually tapering off if she has reached a point in her life where she's trying to establish herself as a person rather than a sex object. Also, when women "find themselves," they also sometimes find the need to come together on a sexual level with a man less pressing. This is due to a sense of identity and self-worth taking place. In other words, she finds she no longer needs sex as a means of proving her value; sex begins to be reoriented, put into another perspective. One woman put this very aptly: "In the early part of my relationship with my husband I wanted sex all the time; I was always ready for him. But, I had nothing else at that time; no interests, no sense of identity. He was my whole life, my reason for being."

Neptune will take the Mars energy and dissolve it in order to reorient it. There is a softening of the hard edges of Mars. Formerly aggressive types can turn into pussycats. A person who is aggressive up to the time of this transit will become softened by the Neptune effect. The exaggerated result may be a total loss of aggressiveness so that the person appears weak, frail and incapable of any meaningful activity or self-defense. Or, in the case of a hard, rational, "macho" type, it may swing to the other end of the pendulum and the aggression may turn into intensely cruel, cold and sadistic responses. Again, this is a means of over-compensating for feelings of vulnerability, incompetence or impotence on *whatever* level.

There may be some difficulty and confusion in taking action, in initiating things. There may also be some fearfulness in beginning any new venture. Feelings of uncertainty regarding the job or what to do with your energy may be a big question. There is a tendency to dissipate the energy either through procrastination (one's ability to *do* is lost) or overindulgences.

Energies may be channeled into philanthropic work; an urge to be of help to others may come about. The need to do "good works" can result, to make your actions helpful and inspirational. Some sort of spiritual or religious work may be undertaken during this transit. This is a "do-gooder" transit. The energies will be transformed by Neptune.

There may be a tendency to act out the role of martyr or to put yourself into circumstances whereby you'll be taken advantage of, martyred in some way. A woman may fall in love with a man who isn't available; she may be attracted to men who are negative and destructive toward her. There can be delusions and deception regarding men in the life.

A person with a less stressful contact will act in a compassionate and gentle manner; the type of person who gives solace to those needing comfort. There's much of the Piscean manner in the actions of Mars being touched by Neptune.

There can be an intense dislike for physical violence because you are so sensitive to it. Seeing a physical fight between two people may make you feel sqeamish because there's an ability to empathize and actually feel the violence in the pit of your stomach.

Your own actions may be deceptive; you may not realize the true motivation lying behind them, or you may be out to deceive others by your actions. "If I do this then they'll think. . . !" There may also be a tendency to avoid physical contact with others due to the sensitizing influence.

Sometimes you don't know what to "do" next; you don't know what to do with your energy so there may be some confusion surrounding your activities. There may be a tendency to overschedule activities so that you tire yourself out. You lose a sense of proportion and can't handle what you've promised to do.

With Neptune transiting Mars, nervous breakdown may occur; it has been known to happen after the transit. This may be the result of tensions building and overloading and then being released when Neptune passes. Alcohol is a danger; heavy drinking or alcohol abuse.

The energies are usually but not always adversely affected when there is a stressful contact; it can be as debilitating as the transit to the Sun.

Jupiter

The planet Jupiter indicates the ability and capacity for personal expansiveness; hence, the ability to extend oneself, to relate—to the world, to individuals, to objects animate and inanimate. It seems to be the indicator of the degree of enthusiasm, optimism and faith of which the individual is capable.

Jupiter and Neptune are sympathetic in many ways. A contact of Neptune to natal Jupiter heightens its spiritual side and the energy may be put into the pursuit of the spiritual side of life. There may be a strong empathy with the "spiritual" and "religious" life.

There may also be a good deal of confusion regarding spiritual and religious concepts and a dissolution of these concepts can take place. Therefore religious or spiritual crises may occur during this transit.

A desire for faraway places may manifest; there is empathy with some foreign land and a desire to go there.

Relationships take on great intensity. There may be involvement in draining relationships, a need or desire to have as many different relationships as possible. Overindulgence of all kinds takes place. Neptune may take away the ability to relate "realistically"—that is, in a manner others can relate to. "God" complexes may arise or a fanatacism regarding some mission or divine purpose may put off others. Spiritual "spouting" is a possible effect and you may become boring or overbearing with your spirituality. This transit can give an evangelical tint to your expression.

With these two planets in contact, addiction may become a real problem; judgment and a sense of proportion are clouded and not to be trusted. "Just one more. . ." can be the straw that breaks the camel's back. Alcohol, drugs and stimulants are best left for another time. There's a tendency to go overboard, enthusiasms run high (and later, dry).

Spiritual insights are obtained, and lost, and found again in another form. These insights are constantly shifting, kaliedoscoping, spilling over one on the other.

The ability to judge is clouded. Judgements regarding relationships are not founded on anything approaching "reality" so you can get tied up with all sorts. There may be continual deception in the areas of relationships.

There may be an inflated sense of well-being, almost manic. This can take you off the deep end if you don't exert some common sense. Feelings of optimism soar, and sometimes there is a complete loss of optimism.

Regarding the financial side of life, there may occur drains or losses especially with the square or opposition. Unsound opportunities for investments in Neptunian projects may be offered; purchases may not give value for money spent. This is an "inflation" contact, especially with a conjunction. Because of expansive feelings, your generosity may be misplaced or misused, as well as your sympathies. The underdog appeals. There can be a desire to be of some help to others, a benevolent or philanthropic attitude may prevail. One tends to become more charitable and giving under the less stressful aspect of this transit. A person tending to egotism and pomposity can be transformed through the "humbling" influence of a Neptune transit. On the other hand, these things may be exaggerated if there's stress.

Saturn

Saturn indicates the areas of the life needing form, structure and discipline; those areas in which things don't come easily! It's the "authority" in the life, and indicates the "weak" point in the life and physical system.

When Neptune contacts natal Saturn there is a keen sensitivity to restrictions and a desire to break all bonds of authority. All reason, commonsense and practicality can fly the coop, as well as fears regarding the area of life being affected by this transit.

For example, a woman under this influence felt for the first time in her life no fear regarding relationship and decided to take a chance at happiness and married. The 7th house was being transited by Neptune. Also, the man she picked for her husband was totally unacceptable to her father (Saturn in the 1st) and she unconsciously broke his influence over her by her choice of a mate.

Neptune has a tendency to dissolve whatever restrictions or reservations you may have been feeling up to this time. There's an urge to break any bonds holding you back from free expression. This is usually done in an unthinking manner; *anything* that will affect the breaking of those bonds is used. You get a taste of freedom and want more, so you attempt to dissolve whatever binds. "Freedoms" experienced at this time are illusory; they aren't what you think they are. It seems great, freedom at last; but you later realize it doesn't last and there are prices to be paid. If there are parental ties in effect during this transit they will be broken, not gently, sometimes with self-destructive methods. If the chart isn't a stressful one, breaks will simply and inexorably come about; this is the time for them.

Confusion regarding responsibilities and duties comes about: Where do they lie? What are they? What is expected of me? Do I really want to take on this responsibility? And so on.

Saturn represents fear and Neptune combining with it can bring unreasoning and irrational fears that can paralyze, especially if Mars is involved in the configuration. Neptune dissolves the structure of Saturn and this can be rather frightening when one senses one's foundations crumbling. But if you keep in mind that through the Neptune effect a new orientation is possible, letting go so the Saturn can be restructured won't be so fearful. It may help you to understand the concept of "letting go" if you think about sitting in a chair. There you are, nice and comfortable in your chair. An hour from now you may still be relatively comfortable in it. But as each hour passes, the chair becomes less and less comfortable until, several hours later, it becomes downright uncomfortable and even painful. Letting go and changing can bring relief. Saturn denotes rigid concepts; where there is rigidity the transit is exaggerated and frightening. Neptune heightens and intensifies, and any Saturn fears will be so affected.

Neptune can also elevate the structure and form which Saturn gives, enhancing and spiritualizing the Saturn placement, freeing it from its rigid nature and softening its influence. Neptune can impart a benevolence to the Saturn expression, making it supportive rather than selfish and demanding, a compassionate teacher rather than a hard-nosed taskmaster. Neptune softens and diffuses, like a soft light, taking away the hard edges. Saturn can use a little of this from time to time.

Since Saturn is the teacher and Neptune is illusion, the two planets work together to show the illusion of freedom: this is why the freedoms which are sought or acquired during this transit don't turn out to be what you thought they were. Saturn is responsibility, Neptune is the desire to be free. You may learn under this one that with freedom comes responsibility, something you may not have been aware of until this time.

Uranus

Uranus indicates the pattern of behavior; the will to be or do; the area of independent behavior and need for freedom of expression, and the area of changefulness in the life.

The contact of Neptune to natal Uranus can bring sudden flashes of spiritual or personal insights and revelations of the "A-HA!" or "Eureka!" variety.

Neptune combining with Uranus will also seek freedom. One's "uniqueness" wants to break out. With Neptune to Saturn there's the urge to break the ties that bind, on whatever level they happen to be operating. With Neptune to Uranus, however, what is sought is freedom in terms of behavior: to be and do what you've always dreamed of being and doing; to behave the complete fool if you're so moved; to be with whomever you wish and wherever you wish without being concerned with what other people are going to think about it. It can be a "maverick" transit, a itation. On the creative side, ingenuity and inventiveness become stimulated and great "discoveries" may come about.
become stimulated and great "discoveries" may come about.

On the stressful side, this one brings worry, especially regarding one's sanity. There may be fantasies of madness, confusion regarding madness, or a fear of nervous breakdown. There is a feeling that illusive changes are taking place that are very hard to pin down, and so you can feel uneasy. There are feelings of instability and a fear of flipping out. There are feelings of intense irritation.

This transit may bring you in contact with mental illness, mental institutions, psychiatry, and so forth. People close to you may become highly erratic in behavior; you may become involved with unstable, "strange," changeable types. Separations from other people can also occur.

Spiritual guidance from another may come with this transit, but it may be on a deceptive level; there may be dishonest intentions on the part of the "messiah." There may be alliances made with people who are very different and unusual from the norm and the outcome of these alliances is totally unpredictable. People come and go in the life but there is always some "spiritual" quality about them, negative or positive.

There can also be confusion regarding goals, not knowing what you want to do in the long run.

Insights and revelations received at this time must be carefully considered and weighed: listen to them, but don't blindly accept them as gospel. The intuitive response is often intensified and heightened.

Neptune

Neptune indicates the ability to envision, to imagine. It is the strength of the imaginative powers and the spiritual and/or psychic perceptions. Its position in the natal chart indicates the areas of likely delusion, illusion, fantasy and daydreaming. It's that nebulous area of the life! Here is where the individual says, "I dream. . . ."

Neptune's first stressful aspect to itself—the square—occurs around age 42. At this time several outer planets are simultaneously forming stressful aspects to themselves:

Jupiter opposition Jupiter during the 40th year;
Saturn opposition Saturn during the 42nd year;
Uranus opposition Uranus during the 39th-40th years.

No wonder this period of life is called the mid-life crisis! And as if this weren't enough to make one aware of needed changes in the life, Pluto comes along to square itself around the 44th year. I call it the "just in case" aspect—just in case the others weren't effective enough to get you on the way to the second half of life.

Since there's so much happening at the time Neptune is squaring itself, it would be folly to try to describe just exactly what its effect is. However, it is well known that during this period of mid-life crisis, one of the things that weighs heavily are the "dreams" of the first half of life—all the things we dreamed of accomplishing. Have we realized them? If not, what happened to them?

There also occurs now—whether or not one wishes to acknowledge it as such—a spiritual crisis. It's especially acute in the materially oriented Western culture.

Much as I should like to dwell on the virtues of Eastern philosophy in regard to this transition phase, I'll hold myself in check. It won't work for the Western psyche anyway.

The spiritual crisis manifests most clearly in the person who has acquired a reasonable degree of material success and says "What's it all mean?" *That* is a spiritual crisis.

Transition periods are always irksome. And this is one of the biggest. All those vague niggling feelings and fears. Where'd I go wrong? What's it all for? What's it all mean? Where do I go from here? Is this all there is?!

Probably because Saturn is lurking around at this time, this is a period of reevaluation in terms of your direction in life. There's an uncanny feeling of deja vu—like you've been here before! It has overtones of the period leading into your 30th year when Saturn conjuncted itself. But this time there's more of a note of urgency. After all, you *are* entering the second half of your life. If it hasn't already made an impression on you, there's no getting around the fact you're mortal. And either you realize playtime's over and you need to get down to some serious business or you begin to understand the *play's* the thing. If you're lucky, you realize the latter. Because the person who has taken action only as a means to an end is the loser in this game. It's the person who realizes the spirit is in the action itself who finds the "secret" of life itself.

This can be, and is for many, one of the most highly creative periods of life. For many parents, child-rearing is ended or nearly so, and this releases new energies. Innate talents and capacities may be realized; lessons from past mistakes have been learned; confidence arises out of experience.

It's well known that many people begin entirely new careers or other enterprises at this time. It's probable that motivation comes through the four planets aspecting themselves. Their message is clearly "Get off your rusty-dusty!" Some feel that time's awastin' and need to at least try to realize some portion of the dream of youth. Also, the dreams of youth get pared down to more realistic and attainable levels—the possible is reshaped into the probable. Unrealistic dreams, aims, hopes, and ambitions receive a sometimes much-needed perspective through what can be an agonizing reevaluation.

This is traditionally the change of life for people. We all experience it in the changing condition of our bodies—a highly unpleasant experience for those who were certain they were immortal. *That's* a spiritual crisis. We are getting older—no doubt about it. There can be a sense of desperation regarding these physical changes, especially regarding one's sexuality. In order to assure themselves of their sexual attractiveness, many women and men seek sexual love affairs, married or not. What easier way to convince yourself you aren't coming apart at the seams? How many men at this time seem urgently compelled to propagate "one more" child? And how many divorces take place at this time? How many men seek a younger woman who can bear the child that is the symbol of the fulfillment of his dream of immortality? Women are coming to the end of their child-bearing years; menopause lurks before them as a spectre of their waning "fruitfulness." A degree of uncertainty regarding their "womanliness" can set in. Many feel they're losing their sex appeal.

And so sex with someone new at this time is like a stimulating injection, like an invigorating tonic. And like all such artificial stimulants, this too eventually loses its efficacy. Neptune's illusions still hold sway here. Trying to hold back time in the arms of a lover is a losing proposition. (It seems the Jupiter opposition Jupiter has something to do with this phenomenon; Neptune helps it along.)

The autumn of life can be far richer than the spring if we become aware of the unsuspected fruit which has grown within. "The winter which follows is not barren if the harvest has been stored, and the withdrawal of sap is only a prelude to a new spring elsewhere." *

*Irene Claremont de Castillejo, "Knowing Woman," Harper & Row, Publishers, 1974, p. 150.

Pluto

In the natal chart, Pluto is the indicator of unconscious motivations, actions born of deep motivation; compulsions and obsessions; and the capacity for personal transformation, or rebirth. I believe it also represents the survival instinct.

I have no reliable information on the transit of Neptune to natal Pluto. However, it would seem that, if Pluto is strong in the natal horoscope, there will have to be very deep stirrings in the unconscious. Whatever has been gestating within Pluto's realm will be dislodged and come to the surface. It may be likened to the growth of a flower, or the rising of garbage to the surface. Both these planets are the Great Dissolvers and if there's a strong tie-in to the Ascendant or Sun there will undoubtedly be dramatic personality changes in the individual. I know that Pluto has a very definite uprooting effect. This suggests to me that *complete* transformation of whatever areas are being affected by these two planets will take place, either totally on the inner level or in conjunction with the outer. This transformation is slow in nature, i.e., it isn't violent or eruptive but more like the evolving of a seed into its final product.

Again, Neptune has a softening effect and therefore Pluto's character, like that of Mars, may be softened. There may be a loss of will with this transit for I think Pluto has a great deal to do with the individual's willpower and survival instinct. My personal experience leads me to conjecture that a stressful transit of Neptune to Pluto, particularly the square, brings death—either on a physical or deep personality level: *if* other transits are condusive and *if* the time is right.

Considerable energy may be channeled into large-scale reformation and regeneration projects, either for the self or for the world in general, if Pluto has a powerful natal position. The lower type of Plutonian energy may be transformed through the spiritualizing and compassionate influence of Neptune.

In regard to the sexual aspect of Pluto, there may be fear or confusion surrounding sex; sexual encounters may become unpleasant or threatening; or there may be a complete transformation or transcendance of the sexual energies. I can't help wondering—and this is mere conjecture on my part—if the influence of Neptune on Pluto might precipitate such a profound change of sexual attitude that its extreme outcome may result in transsexuality.

Those undergoing this transit with Pluto strongly constellated in their charts may take on a charismatic appeal and find they have the ability to mesmerize the public and manipulate large numbers of people. The other side of the coin is that this person may himself become enmeshed in "mob" psychology, "mob" undertakings, mass movements and concepts, particularly of a "religious" or "spiritual" nature.

Neptune Transiting the Houses

*T*he following descriptions of Neptune's transit through the astrological houses are also applicable to Neptune's house position at the time of birth. Its natal house position may be termed "the area of perpetual perplexity," especially if there are stressful aspects from natal Neptune to the personal natal planets. For example, individuals with natal Neptune in the Tenth house are usually uncertain about career aims and have some confusion about their position in the general scheme of things. It may take half a lifetime before the cloudiness surrounding these issues clears up. On the other hand, Neptune transiting the Tenth house will bring this same cloudiness to these issues for most, if not all, of the duration of its transit. When Neptune transits a house, and especially when it's making aspects to the personal natal planets off and on during the transit, this too will be an area of perplexity as well as the areas in which the aspected planets lie. The only difference between the natal and transiting position is (as stated for the planets): the person born with Neptune in a particular house has learned to live with it on some level.

Ascendant

Neptune contacting the Ascendant can bring in a period of intense confusion regarding the personal life, and pie-in-the-sky ambitions. This is a time of grand illusions and delusions of grandeur. You're ready to take the world by the tail. The effect is at times a natural high; consequently its opposite, the low, is abysmal. If you fall in love (a pretty safe bet), it's the love of a lifetime, a love so intense you're sure no one else has ever had such a love. It can be a highly romantic, glamorous period. You may meet many fascinating, strange and very weird people who bring excitement into your life. This is a period of great deception, both of self and from others. And there is an urge to sacrifice the self for a cause, usually out of love or pity. The need for love at this time can be overwhelming and, because of this desperate need, unfortunate relationships are sometimes formed.

There can be sporadic losses of psychological stability; a feeling of losing your grip, and at times not even caring whether you do. You can become unsure of yourself, of your sanity. There is sometimes a feeling you can't make it and a need for someone to take care of you. There may be suicidal moments. There can be an immense fear you can't name, and there's the potential for personality split. One hears inner voices that come to soothe the anguish of fear and uncertainty.

There can be very strong feelings of suffering that go soul deep, an immense sadness that pervades everything. Religious or spiritual longings rise up and can find no satisfaction; you can experience one spiritual/religious crisis after another.

There may be difficulty separating dreams from reality. You begin to wonder on which level you really live; whether you dreamed a situation or it really happened out here. Coming out of the dream state to consciousness is often a confusing transition.

Changes in your lifestyle may come due to confusion. Jobs suddenly become lusterless and unexciting. So you change, or at least want to. The mundane world seems lackluster so you begin to seek the "strange," pursuing the occult and so on. There can be physical dissipation, weight loss, and a very definite danger of involvement in alcohol and drugs; drinking too much or taking drugs in order to escape, or becoming deeply involved with someone who has these problems because you want to "save" them.

Death experiences can occur with this transit; people can physically die and come back to life. Or it may be the death of the personality as it existed up to the time of the transit. If you're ready to go, this is the transit that will take you out.

On a more mundane level, there's a strong attraction to the arts, theater, etc. You may become actively and creatively involved in these things or simply increase your time at the movies. This is certainly a less dangerous form of escape.

Many of the effects of Neptune to the Ascendant can also be applied to the Sun since both these points are strong indicators of the personality and physical body.

Tenth House

What do I do with my life, where do I fit in? seem to be the primary questions of this contact. There will be similarities to the Neptune effect on Saturn: problems with authority—what is it, who and what am I responsible to? There's a need for personal freedom and expression in the work, and a keen sensitivity to your place in the world and much confusion as to exactly where it is. Is terms of career, there is confusion. What do I do with my life? What do I want to do in terms of a career? There's a need to be of some sort of help to the world in general, and a "savior" complex may arise.

There can be delusions of grandeur regarding career, unrealistic aims and goals in that direction. It seems there is more enthusiasm than discipline regarding the career. Perhaps you want the world to simply give it to you without having to work for it; a feeling that the world owes you a living. There's also a sense of not getting proper recognition for your accomplishments. This can give a "Super-Star" complex; or glamor positions are wanted. You definitely don't want to "clean the fish" with this position of Neptune!

I do think this house has something to do with the father, if he was the authority figure in your early life. If so, there will be some confusion regarding him, perhaps a feeling of not knowing who he really is. With the natal placement of Neptune here, there are definite cases where the father was missing in the early childhood or was a "nebulous" character or vague figure. He may become so when Neptune transits this house. We may even say the father may be lost in some way. There may be some confusion regarding both the parents with this transit, especially regarding your responsibilities and duties toward them.

The most important effect is the uncertainty as to where you fit in and your place in the scheme of things. Neptune may show you where and how you're being unrealistic in this area of your life.

Seventh House

Here we have confusion, delusion and illusion in close relationships. There are unrealistic expectations regarding marriage and partnerships; the ideals are so high that nothing on earth will ever come close. The individual may be so sensitive to the whole idea of "marriage" that it's avoided like the plague due to an unreasoning fearfulness. Or the expectations are so high that nothing can be consummated. One seeks the "knight in shining armor" or the "damsel in distress" for a partner. You may marry someone in order to "save" them. The ideas of marriage and of what a marriage partner should be can be overly romantic. There will be a great deal of projection onto the other person—they will be what you want them to be and, therefore, you may experience great difficulty in perceiving them as they really are. People you meet whom you think will be ideal mates turn out to be far less than ideal, so disappointments are overwhelming and plentiful. There's a tendency to blame the other person for turning out to be a creep. The thing is, that person was a creep all along and any of your friends could have told you so, in fact they probably tried to. But you were blinded by "love" and couldn't see or didn't want to see the reality of the situation. You may feel you'll never attain what you believe to be the ideal marriage so you may give up the whole idea. And that's what you need to do—give up the "idea" and deal with things as they are.

Business relationships are often frought with confusion and a certain amount of paranoia. You may wonder if they're out to get you. On the other hand, these partnerships may be of a highly stimulating, creative and inspirational nature if the energies can be directed that way.

It's very difficult to see the "other" with this placement or transit of Neptune. There's a tendency to project your ideas and ideals onto them, to try to make true what you believe, to make your wish come true, to make this dream a reality. You may succeed in creating a nightmare if you refuse to open your eyes.

Fourth House

You might begin to wonder where you come from when Neptune hits this angle; some questions come up regarding your beginnings, or roots, as well as wondering how it will all end. The domestic scene may become a site of confusion. You may set up housekeeping with someone you're infatuated with but don't really know yet and later find yourself in an intolerable atmosphere. Domestic alliances may be made under deceptive conditions.

There may arise the need for glamor and excitement in the area of the home; or your home may take on an aura of glamor and excitement. There may also be a need to retreat and keep your home sacred to yourself, your ivory tower, your sanctuary. There may also arise some fears regarding the home. Or there may be Neptunian problems related to the home or the domestic area: sinking foundations, water or gas leaks; illicit drugs or alcohol problems on the part of a family member. Buying property under this transit is highly suspect; "land deals" and frauds may come into your life.

The atmosphere at home becomes more important; formerly messy habits may now become irritating due to your increased sensitivity to the environment. A revamping of the home, redecorating, making the home more comfortable and relaxing, or even romantic, may result.

The Fourth house has to do with your basic structure, basic foundation, and Neptune comes in and begins its dissolution process in order to reorient things. You may become disillusioned with yourself, with whatever you have built upon up to this point and begin to feel it wasn't what you thought it was.

There may be some draining influence in the home, from leaky pipes to some family members being a drain on your emotions and energies. There will be questions regarding home, domestic and family matters, and some uncertainty regarding these things. Such matters may become worrisome and begin to affect your career because your energies are being drained off into the area of your homelife. You may begin to wonder where your real responsibilities lie: to your family or to your career? You may feel that you want to escape from all "home" responsibilities, just go off somewhere and be by yourself on a desert isle. There may also be an urge to move, or to change your place of residence to some foreign land. The old things become dull and mundane and you feel a need for something more exciting, glittering in your homelife. You want something unusual and dramatic surrounding you. You may even pack your bags and leave your family to go live with someone you think is glamorous and exciting! There may be some sort of loss that brings great sorrow or suffering in the homelife.

The upshot of this transit is a sensitizing to your home environment and need for reorientation.

Second House

Neptune brings in idealism regarding what you do to earn your living, how you'll make your money. Some confusion may crop up as to what your natural talents and resources are. A chance to use the more creative side of your resources as a means of making a living may present itself. You may turn to the arts as a means of making money. There will be an urge to acquire things of a Neptunian nature. What you find desirable to own may change as Neptune moves through this house: it brings in confusion and then a change of values. It may break the illusion of possessions. What was valuable up to this point may now seem shallow or too materialistic. There may be an attempt to acquire the more spiritual aspects of life itself. You may experience drains on your resources or income; delusions regarding income sources; you may be victimized or exploited in some way by an employer.

Third House

As with Neptune's contact to Mercury, when it transits this house there may be some mental confusion, confusion in the area of communication. Daydreaming and problems of concentration, especially when it comes to learning new things, may come about. School or education may present difficulties. Some strange circumstances revolving around siblings and close relatives may crop up; they may put a drain on you because you're more sensitive to them. Travel may be confounding; it may also be glamorous or romantic. You may want to take a sea voyage. This transit is not the best time to buy a used car! Neptune in the third house can be a highly inspirational transit if the aspects are conducive.

Fifth House

Glamor and excitement are sought; you want to be entertained on a grand and lavish scale. Love affairs can be either very confusing and debilitating or very inspirational. Cut and dried sexual encounters are repulsive. There's a need for the romantic element in sexual matters. But there may be a good number of one-night stands with this one due to the confusion. There may also be love affairs of such a high spiritual quality that they are not consummated on the physical level. This is the transit for "other wordly" affairs and "spiritual" sexual relationships. You may also feel that the relationship you have is of such a sublime nature you don't want to put it on a "sordid" level by having sex with the one you love.

There may arise a strong urge to join or become involved in some way with the theater. Neptune's inspiration stirs the natural creative juices; so there may be a release of creativity with this transit.

In the matter of children, there may be unrealistic ideals and romantic ideas about having babies. This may be the "love child" transit. There may also be some vague or unknown fear regarding children or pregnancy. Unwanted pregnancy may also occur. You may not be able to see your children clearly or your sex partner realistically.

Obviously, matters of speculation can be frought with deception.

Sixth House

Neptune transiting this house may urge you to sacrifice yourself to your job so that you become a workaholic. Pay may not be commensurate with energy put out. The job may become draining, and the health may suffer. Now is when undiagnosable physical ailments may show up. It's important to take care of your health with this transit, although there is a tendency to be unaware of it. On the other hand, the job may become highly inspirational and gratifying on a creative level. You'll want to be doing something out of the ordinary. Glamor jobs will appeal. You may become sensitized to your work environment and easily drained if your approach is wrong or if the atmosphere is negative or unhealthy. There may also arise vague circumstances or orders regarding your job may not be understood. You may be promised remuneration and be deceived into applying yourself more energetically to find later there is only a new title with no money coming for your efforts.

There may also be some confusion as to what kind of job you want to engage in; perhaps some daydreaming in this area. There may be a desire to join some "helping" profession, to be of service to humanity.

Eighth House

Neptune brings a sensitivity to the mysteries of life and the occult sciences and arts. This influence may bring you into contact with "psychic" entities, mediumistic occurrences and the like. Psychic phenomena may enthrall and enveigle. Matters of death and the hereafter become fascinating and may become obsessional. There may be death experiences, as with the Neptune contact to the Ascendant. Sex may play a more important part at this time: the "mysteries" of sex and procreation; a tendency to dissipation of the sexual energies; sexual attitudes may undergo a transformation process. There may be periods of sexual impotency due to a draining influence of the psychic or spiritual side of life so there is no energy left over for the physical side of life. Strange sexual encounters may be experienced that may transport you to other dimensions, or so it seems. These encounters can be of an ephemeral and ecstatic type, of such intensity that you feel transported out of space and time. This is also a transit for sexual fantasies. And there can be a good deal of fun with sex. Neptune has its whimsical, impish side, so sex can become playful and "giggly."

There may be deception and delusion in all the above matters as well as in terms of what's coming to you from others. "Inheritances" and the "resources" of those close to you may be lost in some way or not seen realistically. IRS audits have been known to come from "out of the blue." There is also the possibility of cutting loose from "inherited ties."

Those with no former experience or contact with the occult side of life suddenly become fascinated with it. The danger lies in the inexperienced individual going overboard; judgment in these matters is lacking as well as a sense of proportion.

Ninth House

One's sense of ethics, morality, judgments and philosophy are under Neptune's influence, so they are going to experience a dissolution and reorienting. If a material approach has been dominant, this will change and may be uncomfortable until the restructuring takes place. One can go through a period where there is no sense of ethics or morality because these things have been "lost" for the time being; many alternatives are being presented. Religion becomes clouded and confusing: "Is there or isn't there a God?" may be an important theme.

Some of what is said of Neptune to Jupiter can be applied to this transit. Of course, there is always the possibility of great spiritual inspiration and insight coming through this transit; this is the house of the higher mind and it becomes sensitized. Neptune brings the opportunity for transcendental experience.

Eleventh House

If this is the house of goals and ambitions, you're going to wonder what they're all about. Where am I headed? Do I really want that? What direction do I take now? And, where are my friends leading me? For, there's deception and delusion regarding the help you're getting from your friends. Or, they may be truly inspirational. You may begin to wonder who your real friends are or whether or not you truly have any. There's a lot of confusion as to what friends are and what friendship is. But, if you're lucky, friends will bring you inspiration and give you a less materialistic approach or lead you in that direction. They may also try to lead you into irresponsibility. They can also be a draining influence because you're more in sympathy with them; their needs may suck you dry if you allow your sympathies full sway. You can feel their moods and emotions and sometimes wonder which are your own and which belong to them. There's a tendency to over-respond to them and this is how you'll be drained. The underdog and all in need will pull on you. You must protect yourself by channeling your sympathies, by parcelling them out so to speak. If you don't, your time won't be your own. A little selfishness during this transit can be healthy. You may want to sacrifice yourself entirely for some friendship. It won't be worth it.

Twelfth House

In the Twelfth house, Neptune sensitizes the unconscious. Things start getting stirred up deep inside and there can be feelings of "uneasiness" that you can't pinpoint. You're getting ready for a transformation when Neptune approaches your Ascendant in a few years. This is an excellent time to begin any self-analytic projects. Therapy or analysis can bring great rewards over the years of Neptune's transit here. Dreams become more stimulated and there are insights into the deeper layers of yourself and life. Uranus in the Twelfth brings flashes of insight; Neptune brings them about more slowly. This is a period of intense inspiration coming from *inside yourself*.

If Mercury is tied in while this transit is occurring, this is the time of the voices; but they may come without a Mercury tie-in. Listen to them and work with them. You may become very sensitive to the suffering of others and the world in general and go about assuming the sorrowful burdens of others. But it's your own suffering you must look to. You may realize with this transit that you are the one most in need of your sympathy and compassion. As long as you give it to the world you don't have to face your own needs. Look to your own suffering and enlightenment. And then maybe you can help others.

Some Practical Guidelines to a Perplexing Transit

*I*f you're having the transit, the best thing you can do for yourself under a Neptune transit is to listen to music: preferably strings and preferably classical. Your nervous system is so sensitive that anything other than soft, soothing music is going to wipe you out. You need to be recharged and this is where gentle music comes in. It has a healing effect, of this there is absolutely no doubt. It seems to bring together and heal that fragmented and dissolving feeling that comes with Neptune.

You need to be alone from time to time so that you can relax your psychic defenses. One of the reasons Neptune transits are so tiring is that we spend almost all the time erecting and keeping up psychic defenses; otherwise we'd disintegrate. We often do this unconsciously so we aren't aware that this is what is debilitating us. It takes an enormous amount of energy to defend yourself on levels you aren't even aware of. A good deal of physical tension results and this can bring about a "sick" feeling, or flu-like symptoms. Whenever possible, go to a room where you can be alone with yourself. Either be still or listen to soothing music. Allow yourself to flow and merge with the music; you don't have to defend yourself against it. If you feel like crying, cry. If you feel like singing with the music, sing. If you feel like dancing, dance. All these things relieve tension and leave you feeling much more at peace with yourself.

Try not to rationalize everything that is coming into or out of you. Understanding doesn't always come from the intellect. Your guts understand many things your head can't comprehend.

Try to relax and practice going with the natural ebb and flow of your energies. Don't force yourself to do things. Lie down when you feel a need for rest; be alone when you feel you need to. Don't try to explain what's happening to you, not to anyone or even yourself in the beginning. After some time goes by, sometimes months, things begin to coalesce and answers begin forming.

If you're feeling a lack of energy or interest in your surroundings, don't feel guilty. The energy is inside working on another level. That's the area you have to plug into. Pay attention to your dreams and fantasies, and most important, write them down. Get the material up and out of the unconscious so you can take a look at it in the light of day. It may be incomprehensible at first but later it begins to make sense.

If you never drank alcohol before and begin to, or if your drinking increases, don't worry about it but be aware of it. Sometimes you need a good drunk to relieve the tension! Just don't do it every day. A glass of wine before bed can be soothing. And listen to music before bedtime; you'll sleep more peacefully and sometimes dreams are less troubling.

What you are experiencing is for the most part formless and you want to give it form because that's your cultural conditioning. If you're really driven by this urge to give your experiences form, try expressing them in painting, drawing, sculpting, writing, acting, dancing, singing, playing a musical instrument or whatever art form you're drawn to, even if you've never tried any of these things before. You may be no good at it, you may not win any prizes, but that isn't the goal. The important thing is to give your experience creative expression so it doesn't dissipate you or turn to destructive energy.

If someone close to you suggests you may not be in touch

with "reality," maybe you'd better listen to what they have to say and take it into consideration. Use the people around you to "ground" you from time to time. They can help you maintain some perspective which you badly need off and on. Try to find someone you can trust to talk with, to use as a sounding board; someone whose judgment you trust and respect. Sometimes, verbalizing your experience can bring insights.

If you feel particularly distressed, get help from a professional.

Ψ

If you know someone who's having a Neptune transit, be patient. Someday they'll come to! However, there are times when a good hard dose of reality must be introduced into their lives, but you must try to feel the proper timing. They are very sensitive, often selfishly so, and need a good kick in the pants when they get too far off the track of everyday responsibilities. Allow them their time to experience the ineffable; don't constantly interfere. And try not to worry about them; the more you worry the more they will worry because they sense your state. They need support, moral and sometimes physical or financial. However, overprotecting them can result in total debility. A balance is necessary; you must understand the difference between moral support and overprotection.

See to it that they eat properly and slip them some vitamins if you have that kind of influence over them. They can forget about their physical bodies. You sometimes have to remind them to take it easy if you see them overdoing in some way.

If they try to share some of their experiences with you, listen. They need a sounding board; they need to try to verbalize the experience. It may make no sense to you but that isn't what matters. What matters is that they get it out, and with someone who isn't going to judge them for being "weird" or "crazy." Because this is what they are often afraid of, that they may be crazy. Or that if they tell someone what they're going through, they'll be misunderstood and "put away." They do need to talk and the only thing you can do is listen. They don't need advice or answers because it's all coming to them from inside. What they need from time to time is perspective and you might be able to give that to them. If they are experiencing a particularly difficult transit, try to get them to seek help from a professional therapist or analyst, not because you think they're crazy, but because you think they need an objective perspective.